BIBLE WORD SEARCH PUZZLES

BIBLE WORD SEARCH PUZZLES

JOHN HUDSON TINER

BROADMAN PRESS
Nashville, Tennessee

**To
Virda Watson**

4291-09

ISBN: 0-8054-9109-0
Dewey Decimal Classification: 220.076
Subject Heading: BIBLE—CATECHISMS, QUESTION BOOKS

Printed in the United States of America

Introduction

Bible Word Search Puzzles is a fascinating and educational way to have hours of fun when you're riding the bus, waiting on friends, standing in line, or have time to pass. All of the puzzles in this book are self-contained. No reference books are needed, so you can work them anywhere.

Young and old alike will love *Bible Word Search Puzzles.* Each of the exciting puzzles contains hidden words from key passages of the Bible. These favorite verses show God's love for his people and tell the story of salvation. The book is great for the entire family, church youth groups, and individual enjoyment. Knowledge of God's Word is gained through a fun activity.

Three Challenges

Challenge #1: Listed below each key Scripture are the words from that Scripture that have been hidden in the puzzle grid. A hidden word may be spelled in any direction—forward, backward, up, down, or diagonally. But it is always written in a straight line with no spaces between the letters. The hidden words may fall across one another and share a letter. When you find a word, circle it in the puzzle grid and check it from the word list.

Challenge #2: Below the puzzle grid are blanks for the hidden title. Discover the hidden title which is spelled out by some of the uncircled letters in the solved puzzle grid. Letters for the hidden title will not be part of any of the hidden words.

Challenge #3: Test your memory and Bible knowledge by writing or telling about the key Bible passage from memory. Use the search words as a guide. Scripture references are given for all of the puzzles, and you can study the verses to learn more than you are able to recall.

The King James Version is used throughout the book, although some spellings vary, and solutions to all the puzzles are found in the back.

Have fun!

1

Scripture Reference: Genesis 1:1-5

Words:

THE	BEGINNING	GOD
CREATED	HEAVEN	AND
EARTH	WAS	WITHOUT
FORM	VOID	DARKNESS
UPON	FACE	DEEP
SPIRIT	MOVED	WATERS
SAID	LET	THERE
LIGHT	SAW	THAT
GOOD	DIVIDED	FROM
CALLED	DAY	NIGHT
EVENING	MORNING	WERE
FIRST		

Word Search:

```
T F T H G I L I M O R F W
N E V A E H R S D I A S A
F D L D T N R S S D A Y S
I O T A E E O S M O V E D
R G H B T D E P T D T A W
S T Y A E N I H U E U O E
T D W C K G G V A F O M R
A A E R C I I R I M H R E
S N A E N T T N O D T O D
T D D A P H I R N R I F E
H E A T E T N R F I W I L
E E V E N I N G I A N O L
R N H D N V O I D P C G A
E S L G O O D R H G S E C
```

Hidden Title: _ _ _ _ _   _ _ _   _ _   _ _ _ _ _ _ _ _

2

Scripture Reference: Genesis 1:26-31

Words:

SAID	MAKE	IMAGE
LIKENESS	HAVE	DOMINION
FISH	FOWL	CATTLE
EARTH	CREEPING	THING
CREATED	MALE	FEMALE
BLESSED	FRUITFUL	MULTIPLY
REPLENISH	SUBDUE	LIVING
MOVETH	BEHOLD	GIVEN
HERB	BEARING	SEED
TREE	YIELDING	SHALL
MEAT	BEAST	WHEREIN
THERE	LIFE	GREEN
MADE	VERY	GOOD
EVENING	MORNING	SIXTH

Word Search:

```
G O B D L M N H F I S H A K T
L E S E M I A E L W O F A H H
B L N R A V V D E N E V I G E
R D A S E S E I G R F N R F R
E I E H S S T N N E G E B R E
H A M V S E I M M G P N H U C
Y S G E E P N A E L T O N I A
T I L N E N L E E A H I I T T
E B E E I E I N K T T N E F T
P F R L E R I N R I C I R U L
M C I R D S A A G E L M E L E
O S T L H I E E S D G O H D D
V M O R N I N G B A K D W L L
E U D B U S B G I M A G E O M
T E K A M M U L T I P L Y H A
H D E T A E R C S I X T H E L
S E E D Y R E V G O O D E B E
```

Hidden Title: _ _ _   _ _ _ _ _   _ _ _

3

Scripture Reference: Genesis 3:14-21

Words:

SERPENT	BECAUSE	CURSED
ABOVE	CATTLE	EVERY
BEAST	FIELD	BELLY
SHALL	ENMITY	BETWEEN
WOMAN	BRUISE	GREATLY
MULTIPLY	SORROW	CONCEPTION
BRING	FORTH	CHILDREN
DESIRE	HUSBAND	HEARKENED
VOICE	EATEN	WHICH
COMMANDED	SAYING	GROUND
THORNS	THISTLES	SWEAT
BREAD	RETURN	TAKEN
CALLED	MOTHER	LIVING

Word Search:

```
G  N  C  A  L  L  E  D  A  D  B  A  H  G  T
N  W  O  N  V  O  I  C  E  E  B  E  N  N  A
I  O  A  I  R  M  A  N  A  O  A  I  D  I  E
V  M  C  D  T  U  E  S  V  R  Y  S  N  R  W
I  A  V  O  H  P  T  E  K  A  W  E  A  B  S
L  N  E  T  M  N  E  E  S  D  H  L  B  B  O
I  S  R  O  E  M  N  C  R  B  I  T  S  R  R
E  O  F  P  Y  E  A  E  N  B  C  S  U  U  R
F  J  R  I  D  M  Z  N  E  O  H  I  H  I  O
N  E  T  A  E  U  Y  U  D  W  C  H  M  S  W
S  N  E  R  D  L  I  H  C  E  T  T  C  E  M
E  R  Z  T  T  T  D  K  O  U  D  E  F  R  O
B  V  Q  A  H  I  D  N  U  O  R  G  B  I  T
R  L  E  O  A  P  S  H  A  L  L  S  M  S  H
P  R  R  R  U  L  Z  C  A  T  T  L  E  E  E
G  N  E  S  Y  Y  B  E  C  A  U  S  E  D  R
S  Y  L  L  E  B  Y  T  I  M  N  E  K  A  T
```

Hidden Title: _ _ _ _   _ _ _   _ _ _   _ _ _ _ _ _ _

4

Scripture Reference: Genesis 22:9-18

Words:

PLACE	WHICH	ABRAHAM
BUILT	ALTAR	THERE
ORDER	BOUND	ISAAC
STRETCHED	FORTH	KNIFE
ANGEL	CALLED	HEAVEN
FEAREST	SEEING	WITHHELD
LIFTED	LOOKED	BEHIND
CAUGHT	THICKET	HORNS
BURNT	OFFERING	STEAD
JEHOVAH	MOUNT	MYSELF
SWORN	BLESSING	MULTIPLY
STARS	SEASHORE	POSSESS
ENEMIES	NATIONS	EARTH
BLESSED	OBEYED	VOICE

Word Search:

```
T T N U O M L B U R N T E W P D S
E D W H I C H O B T O F I O A F K
C R N A O I T U O H H T S E H N S
A A E I S R I S A K H S T R I O E
A N D H H L N V C H E S E F B N E
S G V E T E O S E S P D E E S R I
I E Y Z H H B L S D R L Y T V O N
K L L F E C D L E O G E A K E W G
N A P J O K T T E G D R U C S S O
C L I E B R F E N S S G I L E E D
A T T A S I T I R E S O D B A I E
U A L R L J R H K T V I W P S M L
G R U T S E R A E F S A N X H E L
H S M H F M A H A R B A E G O N A
T G G F T H I C K E T S N H R E C
T B O U N D D D E S S E L B E X H
N A T I O N S I O F L E S Y M A I
```

Hidden Title: _ _ _ _   _ _   _ _ _ _ _

5

Scripture Reference: Exodus 20:2-17

Words:

BONDAGE	BEFORE	GRAVEN
LIKENESS	HEAVEN	THYSELF
JEALOUS	VISITING	INIQUITY
FATHERS	CHILDREN	FOURTH
GENERATION	SHOWING	THOUSANDS
COMMANDMENTS	GUILTLESS	TAKETH
REMEMBER	SABBATH	SEVENTH
DAUGHTER	MANSERVANT	CATTLE
STRANGER	RESTED	WHEREFORE
BLESSED	HALLOWED	FATHER
MOTHER	GIVETH	COMMIT
ADULTERY	WITNESS	AGAINST
NEIGHBOR		

Word Search:

```
T E N Y L A S W T H O U S A N D S R
S S F R R S S E N E K I L R O M J E
G T O D E E S H I N H T E V I G E T
R P N N R A T N O P F G N X Q N A H
M N T E B E I L F W N O M T O N L G
H I E B M Q M L U A I A F I G G O U
W T A I U D E E R D N N T S U N U A
C T N I G S N T M S A A G R I I S D
H Z T E Y H S A E B R G R E L T E A
I Y O H V G B R M E E E Y H T I R G
L G T D R E V O N M H R G T L S O A
D I D A W A S E R T O E Q A E I F I
R E V Y N T G K A S O C A F S V E N
E E Q T E R O F E R E H W V S W B S
N B L E S S E D B O N D A G E Y N T
T A K E T H T R U O F L B H H N Z U
R E S T E D M O T H E R E L T T A C
C O M M I T D E W O L L A H N Z N Q
```

Hidden Title: _ _ _   _ _ _ _   _ _ _ _   _ _ _

6

Scripture Reference: Psalm 1

Words:

BLESSED	WALKETH	COUNSEL
UNGODLY	STANDETH	SINNERS
SITTETH	SEAT	SCORNFUL
DELIGHT	LORD	MEDITATE
NIGHT	SHALL	LIKE
TREE	PLANTED	RIVERS
WATER	BRINGETH	FORTH
FRUIT	SEASON	LEAF
WITHER	WHATSOEVER	PROSPER
CHAFF	WIND	DRIVETH
AWAY	THEREFORE	STAND
JUDGMENT	CONGREGATION	RIGHTEOUS
KNOWETH	PERISH	

Word Search:

```
W A T E R H H S I T T E T H S E
I W S A P R W T H P C Y P H R E
T A R I J I E G E O N E A N I R
H Y E D N U I V U K R L O O G T
E I N D N N D N E I L I G D H R
R P N U I G S G S O T A N H T E
B R I N G E T H M A S A W D E T
H O S G L T L H G E T T E X O A
T S T O S L C E E S N S A C U T
E P I D T R R D T R S T H H S I
V E U L M G E A K E E A L H W D
I R R Y N T N V L K F F D O Z E
R R F O N D B B I F T L O E R M
D M C A E L U F N R O C S R S D
C A L T H G I L E D N O S A E S
X P H K N O W E T H L I K E A V
I X H T R O F A E L B E W W T B
```

Hidden Title: _ _ _ _ _   _ _   _ _ _ _ _   _ _ _ _ _

7

Scripture Reference: Psalm 8

Words:

EXCELLENT	EARTH	GLORY
HEAVENS	MOUTH	BABES
SUCKLINGS	ORDAINED	STRENGTH
BECAUSE	THINE	MIGHTEST
STILL	ENEMY	AVENGER
CONSIDER	FINGERS	STARS
MINDFUL	VISITEST	LITTLE
LOWER	ANGELS	CROWNED
HONOR	DOMINION	WORKS
HANDS	THINGS	SHEEP
BEASTS	FIELD	WHATSOEVER
PASSETH	THROUGH	PATHS

Word Search:

```
G L O R R S Y O R D A I N E D S
O F G A R E D I S N O C O D F K
T Y B A N E W D L U F D N I M R
Q N T E N G O O T S S A E A E O
T S E W C M E Q L U I L G V S W
V S O L I A X L C T D P E H T A
H R E N L E U K S S B O S O R V
C E I T L E L S A E S B R N E E
Y O A T I I C H E T M E E O N N
N M T V N S E X A H O A G R G G
X I E G E A I H E G U S N S T E
L S S N R N W V E I T T I G H R
M E H T E S S A P M H S F N D Z
H B H U T H R O U G H L L I T S
H A N D S G L O R Y P E E H S S
B B N W Y T H I N E D S H T A P
```

Hidden Title: _ _ _ _ _   _ _   _ _ _

8

Scripture Reference: Psalm 23

Words:

SHEPHERD	SHALL	MAKETH
GREEN	PASTURES	LEADETH
BESIDE	STILL	WATERS
RESTORETH	PATHS	RIGHTEOUSNESS
THOUGH	THROUGH	VALLEY
SHADOW	DEATH	STAFF
COMFORT	PREPAREST	TABLE
BEFORE	PRESENCE	ENEMIES
ANOINTEST	RUNNETH	SURELY
GOODNESS	MERCY	FOLLOW
DWELL	HOUSE	

Word Search:

```
A S H O N S F O L L O W S T S
G Y S T O F E D D A V S P A H
I C R D A C W I L E E C R B A
D R E H P E H S M N D G E L D
J E T C L S D S S E N D P E O
L M A L A E E U T T N B A C W
D E W S D N O R H A E E R N R
L X A I U E O R U F F N E E V
D L S D T R O I O T E F S S L
M E A H E U E R N E S T T E T
B Z G H G T E L R T O A X R R
K I I H S B H G Y R E W P P O
R N U G O O D N E S S S A T F
R U N N E T H T E L L I T S M
J T H O U G H T E K A M H X O
V A H Y E L L A V H O U S E C
```

Hidden Title: _ _ _ _ _ _ _ _ _ _ _ _ _

9

Words:

UNTO	THEE	LORD
LIFT	SOUL	TRUST
ASHAMED	ENEMIES	TRIUMPH
OVER	NONE	THAT
WAIT	THEM	WHICH
TRANSGRESS	WITHOUT	CAUSE
SHOW	WAYS	TEACH
PATHS	REMEMBER	TENDER
MERCIES	LOVING	KINDNESSES
THEY	HAVE	BEEN
EVER	SINS	YOUTH
TRANSGRESSIONS	ACCORDING	

Word Search:

```
C T R E V A H T U S S A W T
S A T F I L A R S R S S I I
N N U T H H E E E E E H T L
E O O S T M R V R D S A H R
E D R I E G O E R B S M O E
H D H M S E I M E N E E U D
T O B N T S U R T W N D T N
H E A Z P Y E C T A D E C E
R R S A C C O R D I N G E T
T W T E B I I U G T I Q K B
O H H S I U O N T S K H Y M
S L H I M C I T I H N O N E
C O O P C V R N N T E A C H
W R H U O H S E L U O S R T
L D T L W A Y S M T H E Y T
```

Hidden Title: _ _ _ _ _   _ _   _ _ _   _ _ _ _

10

Scripture Reference: Proverbs 6:16-19

Words:

THESE	THINGS	DOTH
LORD	HATE	SEVEN
ABOMINATION	UNTO	PROUD
LOOK	LYING	TONGUE
HANDS	THAT	SHED
INNOCENT	BLOOD	HEART
DEVISETH	WICKED	IMAGINATIONS
FEET	SWIFT	RUNNING
MISCHIEF	FALSE	WITNESS
SPEAKETH	LIES	SOWETH
DISCORD	AMONG	BRETHREN

Word Search:

```
E  S  E  I  L  S  E  V  D  R  O  L  S  E
U  N  T  F  E  I  H  C  S  I  M  N  H  U
G  N  D  I  S  C  O  R  D  H  O  A  T  N
N  I  O  H  I  S  G  D  N  I  T  S  E  T
O  S  T  I  E  N  E  N  T  E  S  S  S  O
T  O  D  V  T  K  N  A  I  O  G  E  I  S
D  H  E  N  C  A  N  O  W  Y  P  N  V  B
T  N  E  I  A  I  N  E  C  R  L  T  E  R
H  G  W  S  G  H  T  I  O  E  O  I  D  E
I  D  H  A  E  H  A  U  M  T  N  W  S  T
N  A  M  O  N  G  D  T  B  O  E  T  W  H
G  I  R  U  N  N  I  N  G  L  B  E  I  R
S  H  E  A  R  T  L  O  O  K  O  A  F  E
T  A  H  T  E  K  A  E  P  S  E  O  T  N
S  S  H  E  D  T  U  E  S  L  A  F  D  A
```

Hidden Title: _ _ _ _ _   _ _ _ _ _ _   _ _ _   _ _ _ _ _

11

Scripture Reference: Ecclesiastes 9:11-12

Words:

RETURNED	UNDER	THAT
RACE	SWIFT	BATTLE
STRONG	NEITHER	BREAD
WISE	RICHES	UNDERSTANDING
FAVOR	SKILL	TIME
CHANCE	HAPPENETH	THEM
ALSO	KNOWETH	FISHES
TAKEN	EVIL	BIRDS
CAUGHT	SONS	SNARED
WHEN	FALLETH	SUDDENLY
UPON		

Word Search:

```
S T R O N G F I S H E S B
S U C L C E R E S S T D R
G A N D L E K S F H A E E
R N I S D I N A A L H N A
I C I N U A K T T T E R D
C A U D R D E S E U C U R
H U B E N C D N W F A T H
E G D I N A E E A I R E T
S H T A R P T V N O F R E
O T H I P D O S M L S T L
N C E A M R S E R N Y L L
S L H R R E H T I E N U A
K N O W E T H B F H D W F
P Q E V I L E S I W S N P
P U E E L T T A B N O P U
```

Hidden Title: _ _ _ _ _ _ _ _ _ _ _ _ _ _ _ _ _

12

Scripture Reference: Ecclesiastes 11:9 to 12:2

Words:

REJOICE	YOUTH	HEART
CHEER	DAYS	WALK
WAYS	THINE	SIGHT
EYES	KNOW	THESE
THINGS	BRING	JUDGMENT
THEREFORE	REMOVE	SORROW
AWAY	EVIL	FLESH
CHILDHOOD	VANITY	REMEMBER
CREATOR	COME	YEARS
DRAW	NIGH	HAVE
PLEASURE	LIGHT	MOON
STARS	DARKENED	CLOUDS
RETURN	RAIN	

Word Search:

```
V  H  T  S  E  S  T  R  A  E  H  E  T  T
O  A  Y  H  D  Y  K  N  I  A  R  H  H  H
W  A  N  U  G  N  E  T  T  U  I  E  D  G
D  F  O  I  O  I  H  S  S  N  R  H  E  I
R  L  H  W  T  I  S  A  E  E  K  E  N  N
C  E  Y  A  N  Y  E  O  F  U  L  J  E  S
C  S  B  G  V  L  N  O  E  N  A  U  K  O
E  H  S  M  P  E  R  E  G  V  W  D  R  R
V  S  I  H  E  E  U  O  M  U  O  G  A  R
I  L  D  L  L  M  T  I  O  O  V  M  D  O
L  W  A  R  D  R  E  J  O  I  C  E  E  W
Y  O  U  T  H  H  R  R  N  C  E  N  P  R
G  N  I  R  B  V  O  L  I  G  H  T  K  S
R  O  T  A  E  R  C  O  S  R  A  E  Y  K
S  T  A  R  S  B  X  M  D  M  U  A  E  T
Y  A  W  A  T  H  E  S  E  T  W  S  J  R
```

Hidden Title: _ _ _   _ _ _   _ _ _ _ _   _ _ _ _ _ _   _ _ _ _

13

Scripture Reference: Isaiah 53:2-3

Words:

SHALL	GROW	BEFORE
TENDER	PLANT	ROOT
GROUND	HATH	FORM
COMELINESS	WHEN	THERE
BEAUTY	THAT	SHOULD
DESIRE	DESPISED	REJECTED
SORROWS	ACQUAINTED	WITH
GRIEF	WERE	FACES
FROM	ESTEEMED	

Word Search:

```
D S U F E R O O T F E N
E E R S F R W I T H I E
R N S R H E E D G C A H
I N O I R O N H O A B W
S M D O P U U M T C E G
E W F E O S E L T Q A S
D E E R S L E H D U U W
B L G R I T A D F A T O
R E D N E T E O O I Y R
R Y E H S G D E R N R R
S S T H W O R G M T D O
S A A R E J E C T E D S
H L I T N A L P W D D E
L S E C A F E I R G B L
```

Hidden Title: _ _ _ _ _ _ _ _ _   _ _ _   _ _ _ _ _

14

Scripture Reference: Daniel 3:19-25

Words:

NEBUCHADNEZZAR	CHANGED	AGAINST
SHADRACH	MESHACH	ABEDNEGO
THEREFORE	SPAKE	COMMANDED
SHOULD	FURNACE	SEVEN
TIMES	HEATED	MIGHTY
BURNING	FIERY	BOUND
THEIR	COATS	GARMENTS
MIDST	BECAUSE	COMMANDMENT
URGENT	EXCEEDING	FLAME
THREE	ASTONISHED	HASTE
COUNSELORS	ANSWERED	LOOSE
WALKING	FOURTH	

Word Search:

```
A  R  H  A  S  T  E  X  C  E  E  D  I  N  G  G
S  B  A  E  E  R  H  T  S  N  I  A  G  A  N  F
Y  H  E  Z  F  U  R  N  A  C  E  O  U  I  H  R
R  T  O  D  Z  M  F  O  U  R  T  H  K  E  E  N
E  H  I  U  N  E  M  N  M  T  H  L  E  G  A  F
I  E  N  U  L  E  N  I  R  N  A  A  E  A  T  D
F  I  C  E  S  D  G  D  B  W  T  E  S  R  E  E
C  R  G  H  V  H  F  O  A  N  K  T  U  M  D  H
M  O  A  N  T  E  U  W  E  H  H  I  A  E  C  S
I  C  U  Y  I  N  S  M  D  E  C  C  C  N  O  I
H  W  A  N  D  N  D  E  R  M  N  U  E  T  M  N
T  I  M  E  S  N  R  E  K  A  P  S  B  S  M  O
H  P  H  T  A  E  F  U  F  L  A  M  E  E  A  T
Z  O  A  M  W  O  L  U  B  T  S  D  I  M  N  S
A  O  M  S  R  Q  C  O  C  H  A  N  G  E  D  A
C  O  N  E  A  H  C  A  R  D  A  H  S  Z  E  D
C  A  T  N  E  G  R  U  E  S  O  O  L  X  D  I
```

Hidden Title: _ _ _ _   _ _ _   _ _   _ _ _   _ _ _ _ _ _ _

15

Scripture Reference: Matthew 3:13-17

Words:

THEN	JESUS	GALILEE
JORDAN	JOHN	BAPTIZED
FORBADE	SAYING	HAVE
NEED	ANSWERING	SAID
BECOMETH	FULFIL	RIGHTEOUSNESS
SUFFERED	WHEN	WENT
STRAIGHTWAY	WATER	HEAVENS
OPENED	SPIRIT	DESCENDING
LIKE	DOVE	LIGHTING
VOICE	HEAVEN	BELOVED
WHOM	WELL	PLEASED

Word Search:

```
Y J E S N M O H W D U S I S
J A B P A E P T E E D I R D
O Z W D L D V Z E E L I D E
H S E T E E I A V I G L S S
N E P N H T A O E H G F N C
N S E I P G L S T H N O A E
W P N A R E I E E A I R D N
O H B E B I O A G D R B R D
B L E H V U T A R N E A O I
T E A N S A L P K T W D J N
N V C N D I E X D A S E L G
E G E O L I G H T I N G I F
W S V E M N G N I Y A S K O
S E E D D E R E F F U S E V
J E S U S H T Z F U L F I L
R E T A W T Q H V O I C E B
```

Hidden Title: _ _ _ _ _   _ _   _ _ _ _ _ _ _ _ _

16

Scripture Reference: Matthew 5:1-12

Words:

MULTITUDES	MOUNTAIN	DISCIPLES
OPENED	MOUTH	TAUGHT
BLESSED	POOR	SPIRIT
KINGDOM	HEAVEN	MOURN
COMFORTED	MEEK	INHERIT
EARTH	HUNGER	THIRST
RIGHTEOUSNESS	FILLED	MERCIFUL
OBTAIN	PURE	HEART
PEACEMAKERS	CHILDREN	PERSECUTED
REVILE	MANNER	EVIL
AGAINST	FALSELY	REJOICE
EXCEEDING	GREAT	REWARD

Word Search:

```
H E A R T R S K T B R R E A S C
N T D I B P E I E E T E U S E O
D E E I I L R W V E X G E S D M
K T V R S E E I A C M N M V U F
K S I A H C L S E R S U A T T O
I T R N E E I E S U D H N A I R
N S I E R H D P O E P T N U T T
G N Z U K I B E L E D U E G L E
D I P J N A T A R E D O R H U D
O A T G Y H M S B E S M F T M T
M G U H G L E E N I A T N U O M
T A X I I C E E C H I L D R E N
A E R A U R P S W A O B T A I N
E A R T H O S A L R E J O I C E
R D E L L I F T K A Z P R O O P
G D N R U O M K L U F I C R E M
```

Hidden Title: _ _ _ _ _ _ _ _ _ _

17

Scripture Reference: Matthew 6:5-15

Words:

PRAYEST	HYPOCRITES	STANDING
SYNAGOGUES	CORNERS	STREETS
VERILY	THEIR	REWARD
ENTER	CLOSET	FATHER
SECRET	OPENLY	REPETITIONS
HEATHEN	THINK	HEARD
SPEAKING	KNOWETH	THINGS
MANNER	HEAVEN	HALLOWED
KINGDOM	EARTH	DAILY
BREAD	FORGIVE	DEBTORS
TEMPTATION	DELIVER	POWER
GLORY	HEAVENLY	TRESPASSES

Word Search:

```
G E G P S R A R M Y E S R F O S
N V D L R N I C R A Y D R A E H
I I E B O E O E L N N R E S L I
D G B H H R W I A O E N S V S E
N R T T Y A Y G T V S A E E V T
A O O E R P O L I I P E C R H R
T F R D K G O L N S T R T I S M
S D S R U N E C E E E E N L A T
Q N X E E D O R R T V G P Y C E
Y D S V U H T W E I S A B E S M
Y L N E P O T M E U T R E T R P
K I N G D O M A W T E E S H E T
S P E A K I N G F A H E S Y N A
L S T R E E T S D F Y N M L R T
V D O D E W O L L A H T R I O I
N E H T A E H T R A E E Q A C O
T H I N K K D P O W E R Q D Z N
```

Hidden Title: _ _ _ _ _ _   _ _ _   _ _ _ _ _ _ _ _ _

18

Scripture Reference: Matthew 13:3-8

Words:

SPAKE	MANY	PARABLES
SAYING	BEHOLD	SOWER
WENT	FORTH	SEEDS
FELL	WAYSIDE	FOWLS
CAME	DEVOURED	STONY
PLACES	WHERE	THEY
MUCH	EARTH	FORTHWITH
SPRUNG	BECAUSE	DEEPNESS
SCORCHED	ROOT	WITHERED
THORNS	CHOKED	GOOD
GROUND	BROUGHT	FRUIT
HUNDREDFOLD	SIXTYFOLD	THIRTYFOLD

Word Search:

```
P A R F E L L A B L E O W G T
S S P A K E G N I Y A S A R H
F I R T H S F R U I T H Y O E
H T X T H C N D O O G C S U Y
H U R T H D E R E S S U I N W
O O N O Y R L P O S I M D D H
F B K D E F A O E H P D E L E
F E R H R R O N H L T L S E R
D O T O A E P L A E Y O D S E
W I W B U E D C D N B F E U W
W T L L E G E F A S K Y V A O
Z E G D S S H M O T L T O C S
S P R U N G T T O L H R U E E
D L D E H C R O C S D I R B M
S D E E S M R T N E W H E N A
F O R T H W I T H Y E T D G C
```

Hidden Title: _ _ _ _ _ _ _ _ _ _ _ _ _ _ _ _ _

19

Scripture Reference: Mark 3:14-19

Words:

ORDAINED	TWELVE	SEND
THEM	FORTH	PREACH
POWER	HEAL	SICKNESSES
CAST	DEVILS	SIMON
SURNAMED	PETER	JAMES
ZEBEDEE	JOHN	BROTHER
BOANERGES	SONS	THUNDER
ANDREW	PHILIP	BARTHOLOMEW
MATTHEW	THOMAS	ALPHEUS
THADDEUS	CANAANITE	JUDAS
ISCARIOT	BETRAYED	

Word Search:

```
J E S U S A P P C O I S N P
P T S D E N I A D R O U S E
I W A U P O N S Z T S E R T
L B E T R A Y E D E T D E E
I L E M A N B S S H H D D R
H S E N O E A S E N O A N S
P K I V D L E M N M M H U B
D T B E L N O S E O A T H O
E E E R K E U H W D S J T A
M Z V C O E W E T S I M O N
A H I I H T R T C R C L C E
T S E P L D H J U D A S I R
T W L A N S R E W O P B I G
H A D A L T O I R A C S I E
E P R E A C H N H T R O F S
W S E N D T S A C J O H N G
```

Hidden Title: _ _ _ _ _   _ _ _ _ _ _ _ _   _ _ _ _ _ _ _ _

20

Scripture Reference: Luke 2:8-11

Words:

THERE	WERE	SAME
COUNTRY	SHEPHERDS	ABIDING
FIELD	KEEPING	WATCH
OVER	THEIR	FLOCK
NIGHT	ANGEL	LORD
CAME	UPON	THEM
GLORY	SHONE	ROUND
ABOUT	THEY	SORE
AFRAID	SAID	UNTO
FEAR	BEHOLD	GOOD
TIDINGS	GREAT	WHICH
SHALL	PEOPLE	BORN
THIS	CITY	DAVID
SAVIOUR	CHRIST	

Word Search:

```
D S D L O H E B W N O P U W O
S A F E A R G H E A R M E H T
K I V P H L E R D S T O H I N
E D E I O E L L A H S C B C U
E A Y R D E R R A S B O H H U
P T Y R M T H E I R S C I T Y
I W J A T E E H H D T H G I N
N E S S R N T T R T U S L F A
G R A O R L U E U G R E A T X
W E S B E O H O A O T L C L F
G V E G I P U E C I B H D D L
E O N M E D L N D S R A L I O
N A O H A P I I D I N O E A C
O R S D O C N N S J R B I R K
H T H E Y G C T G D R D F F O
S M P M S H S A V I O U R A D
```

Hidden Title: _ _ _ _ _ _ _ _ _   _ _ _ _   _ _ _ _ _   _ _ _ _ _

21

Scripture Reference: Luke 4:1-13

Words:

RETURNED	JORDAN	SPIRIT
WILDERNESS	TEMPTED	NOTHING
AFTERWARD	HUNGERED	COMMAND
ANSWERED	SAYING	WRITTEN
TAKING	MOUNTAIN	SHOWED
KINGDOMS	MOMENT	DELIVERED
WORSHIP	BEHIND	BROUGHT
JERUSALEM	PINNACLE	TEMPLE
ANGELS	CHARGE	TEMPTATION
DEPARTED	SEASON	

Word Search:

```
G N S A T T D A M N M S C W B T
N O O E M E I E P O T M O R R D
I S S I W A L R U J W O M I O E
H A E O T A F N I I S D M T U R
T E H U S A T T L P S G A T G E
O S R U O A T D E B S N N E H V
N U R A I B E P E R W I D N T I
J E B N E R W G M T W K E X M L
J N K H N O N D I E P A D L O E
T T I E R A E L M K T M R Q M D
G N S S D R S A Y I N G E D E I
D S H R E P I N N A C L E T N F
K I O W S D E T R A P E D H T F
P J S L E G N A H U N G E R E D
G N I K A T D E N R U T E R L V
A T E M P L E C H A R G E B J T
```

Hidden Title: _ _ _ _ _   _ _ _ _ _ _   _ _ _ _ _

22

Scripture Reference: Luke 10:25-37

Words:

CERTAIN	LAWYER	TEMPTED
SAYING	MASTER	INHERIT
ETERNAL	WRITTEN	ANSWERING
NEIGHBOR	WILLING	JUSTIFY
HIMSELF	JERUSALEM	JERICHO
THIEVES	STRIPPED	RAIMENT
WOUNDED	DEPARTED	LEAVING
PRIEST	PASSED	LEVITE
LOOKED	SAMARITAN	JOURNEYED
COMPASSION	WOUNDS	POURING
BROUGHT	SHOWED	

Word Search:

```
W  S  R  D  H  T  O  G  N  I  V  A  E  L  J
T  A  A  E  I  S  H  M  Y  N  E  I  G  E  U
I  Y  I  D  N  W  R  I  T  T  E  N  R  H  S
R  I  M  N  A  B  O  R  E  O  S  U  X  J  T
E  N  E  U  T  C  C  R  F  V  S  E  G  O  I
H  G  N  O  I  E  O  L  O  A  E  N  I  U  F
N  P  T  W  R  J  E  M  L  B  I  S  Q  R  Y
I  F  J  T  A  S  E  E  P  R  H  L  B  N  P
S  I  A  Z  M  R  M  R  E  A  A  G  E  E  Q
D  I  F  I  A  A  E  W  I  N  S  H  I  Y  N
N  E  H  G  S  S  S  Y  R  C  Q  S  Q  E  Y
U  A  T  T  W  N  D  E  W  O  H  S  I  D  N
O  D  E  P  A  R  T  E  D  A  A  O  L  O  I
W  R  Q  P  M  E  G  N  I  L  L  I  W  W  N
Y  P  A  S  S  E  D  G  N  I  R  U  O  P  O
B  R  O  U  G  H  T  D  E  P  P  I  R  T  S
L  E  V  I  T  E  D  E  K  O  O  L  A  Z  R
```

Hidden Title: _ _ _   _ _   _ _   _ _ _ _ _ _ _ _

23

Scripture Reference: Luke 15:11-24

Words:

YOUNGER	PORTION	GOODS
DIVIDED	LIVING	GATHERED
JOURNEY	COUNTRY	WASTED
SUBSTANCE	RIOTOUS	FAMINE
JOINED	HIMSELF	CITIZEN
FIELDS	SWINE	FILLED
BELLY	HUSKS	HIRED
SERVANTS	BREAD	ENOUGH
SPARE	PERISH	HUNGER
ARISE	SINNED	HEAVEN
WORTHY	CALLED	COMPASSION
KISSED	BRING	SHOES
FATTED	MERRY	ALIVE
FOUND		

Word Search:

```
A C F L O S H I M S E L F T C B
F S A O C Y L L E B N X G D O R
I L T L B I H U S K S L J E U I
E D T F L W T P O R T I O N N N
L A E E F E F I I S E N N N T G
D E D I V I D O Z Y P O V I R N
S R G I L E T E H E I A O S Y I
T B L L S O S I C S N G R E O V
N A E S U I R D S N I G N E U I
A D I S R E E A E H A R U U N L
V K E A D N P Y G T U T E P G S
R R E N I M A F H O S N S P E E
E C O O O U R E J T O A G B R O
S L J C Y R R E M U R D W E U H
S W I N E E N O U G H O S W R S
F O U N D N E V A E H A W T X T
```

Hidden Title: _ _ _ _ _ _ _ _

51

24

Scripture Reference: Luke 23:33-38

Words:

PLACE	CALLED	CALVARY
CRUCIFIED	MALEFACTORS	RIGHT
HAND	LEFT	THEN
SAID	JESUS	FATHER
FORGIVE	THEM	KNOW
WHAT	PARTED	RAIMENT
CAST	LOTS	PEOPLE
STOOD	BEHOLDING	RULERS
DERIDED	SAYING	SAVED
OTHERS	HIMSELF	CHRIST
SOLDIERS	MOCKED	OFFERING
VINEGAR	KING	JEWS
WRITTEN	OVER	LETTERS
LATIN	HEBREW	

Word Search:

```
Y R A V L A C P A R T E D O P L
N T S I R H C S A I D S T O L A
R O B E H O L D I N G H C I N T
E C I T O S E O A N E S R F S I
L C H T A F H H E R R P U A R N
K E A Y P I F T S O K E C R E I
M N I L M I T E T F I O I E I E
T N O S P I R C R I N P F H D M
G H E W R R A C L I G L I T L O
T L G W W F A T S E N E E A O C
F A S I E R E G H B T G D F S K
T K H L R A V I E E U T L R W E
F L A W B I I E D N N S E C E D
E M D M E M G C M C I L T R J I
L Z K C H E R E V O U V D O S Y
J E S U S N O D E R I D E D O I
D E V A S T F D E L L A C O Z D
```

Hidden Title: _ _ _ _ _ _ _ _ _ _ _ _ _ _ _ _ _ _ _ _

25

Scripture Reference: Luke 24:1-9

Words:

FIRST	EARLY	MORNING
SEPULCHRE	BRINGING	SPICES
PREPARED	CERTAIN	OTHERS
FOUND	STONE	ROLLED
ENTERED	JESUS	PERPLEXED
THEREABOUT	BEHOLD	STOOD
SHINING	GARMENTS	AFRAID
BOWED	THEIR	FACES
EARTH	LIVING	RISEN
SPAKE	GALILEE	SAYING
DELIVERED	HANDS	SINFUL
CRUCIFIED	THIRD	REMEMBERED
WORDS	RETURNED	

Word Search:

```
J D O D E R A P E R P Y L R A E
S E E T E S E T T G A L I L E E
T W R P H I H T U S S F O U N D
O O E L E E F D U J R I A S V E
N B M D I R R I E R S I T C A E
E T E R E I P S C T N N F D E Q
Q N M K H R U L H U E E E E S
A D B T A S E E E M R R D M R N
B I E U Z P R T R X E C D O H I
E A R T H E S A N V E E R R C A
H R E H A H G D I E L D I N L T
O F D B I H O L G L N Y S I U R
L A O N A O E W O R D S E N P E
D U I N T D B R I N G I N G E C
T N D S G N I V I L U F N I S L
G S S E C I P S A G N I Y A S W
```

Hidden Title: _ _ _ _ _   _ _ _ _ _

26

Scripture Reference: John 3:16-21

Words:

LOVED	WORLD	GAVE
ONLY	BEGOTTEN	WHOSOEVER
BELIEVETH	SHOULD	PERISH
HAVE	EVERLASTING	LIFE
SENT	THROUGH	MIGHT
SAVED	ALREADY	BECAUSE
BELIEVED	NAME	THIS
CONDEMNATION	LIGHT	DARKNESS
RATHER	THAN	THEIR
DEEDS	EVIL	EVERY
HATETH	NEITHER	REPROVED
TRUTH	MADE	MANIFEST

Word Search:

```
G O S L D H T T L B L D O V E
S A I E T L H H E I L E B H H
N F H E N R O L G L V V E S A
E O T W O T I V D I G E C I V
R A I U H E S L E N M I A R E
H A G T V O R E I D S L U E P
Y H T E A O S T F A E E S P B
D O T H W N S O V I P B E N E
A H L E E A M E E E N G X A G
E V A G L R D E S V E A Z M O
R E Y R E V E Z D X E E M E T
L P E G I C S S E N K R A D T
A V R E P R O V E D O N L Y E
E N E I T H E R D A D C I A N
D L U O H S J L I G H T U R T
R I E H T M A D E T H A N N H
```

Hidden Title: _ _ _   _ _ _ _ _   _ _ _   _ _ _ _ _ _

27

Words:

TIBERIAS	MULTITUDE	FOLLOWED
MIRACLES	DISEASED	MOUNTAIN
DISCIPLES	PASSOVER	COMPANY
PHILIP	ANSWERED	HUNDRED
PENNYWORTH	SUFFICIENT	ANDREW
BROTHER	BARLEY	LOAVES
FISHES	NUMBER	THOUSAND
THANKS	DISTRIBUTED	FILLED
GATHER	FRAGMENTS	GATHERED
TWELVE	BASKETS	REMAINED

Word Search:

```
P F O O D F D D R L S O R D D T
I F I V E E I E O E T H B E F N
L O U S R S V A H A N R T R R E
I D L D E O V S M G O U N E A I
H A N A S E I U I T B X Z W G C
P U S S S F L I H I W Z K S M I
H E A G A T H E R E D X E N E F
D P H F I S R T X J J B T A N F
O H V T N U S D N A S U O H T U
M W U T R I S A I R E B I T S S
T D Z P D O A Y Y S L O C A Q B
E V L E W T W T W E C Y O S F A
S K N A H T S Y N E L I M L I S
M I R A C L E S N U R R P H L K
D E W O L L O F R N O D A L L E
V V R E M A I N E D E M N B E T
N U M B E R E H T A G P Y A D S
```

Hidden Title: _ _ _ _   _ _ _   _ _ _ _   _ _ _ _ _ _ _ _

28

Scripture Reference: John 14:1-7

Words:

YOUR	HEART	TROUBLED
BELIEVE	ALSO	FATHER
HOUSE	MANY	MANSIONS
WERE	WOULD	HAVE
TOLD	PREPARE	PLACE
WILL	COME	AGAIN
RECEIVE	UNTO	MYSELF
THAT	WHERE	THERE
WHITHER	KNOW	THOMAS
SAID	LORD	THOU
GOEST	JESUS	TRUTH
LIFE	COMETH	KNOWN
SHOULD	FROM	

Word Search:

```
U C O T A H T M S M F T H L
G O T K N O W N H A O H A O
E O H R H R T W O N K E V R
P R E T O T F O U S W R E D
R L A S B U U E L I D E L I
E E A P T E B R D O I V R S
V E R C E L S L T N A S A E
I C O M E R I U E S S M H W
E H E A R T P F O D O T O B
C W H I T H E R E H E U E F
E R E H T A F R T M L L S L
R N I A G A E Y O D I Y U E
O S L A Z H O C V E N N S S
T O L D W U V G V A T B E Y
L L I W R V N E M O R F J M
```

Hidden Title: _ _ _ _ _ _ _ _   _ _ _   _ _ _ _ _ _ _ _ _

29

Scripture Reference: John 18:3-9

Words:

JUDAS	HAVING	RECEIVED
OFFICERS	CHIEF	PRIESTS
PHARISEES	LANTERNS	TORCHES
WEAPONS	JESUS	THEREFORE
KNOWING	THINGS	SHOULD
COME	SAID	THEM
WHOM	SEEK	THEY
ANSWERED	NAZARETH	WHICH
BETRAYED	STOOD	BACKWARD
FELL	GROUND	THESE
THEIR	SAYING	MIGHT
FULFILLED	SPAKE	GAVEST
LOST	NONE	

Word Search:

```
K J E S U S H S N O P A E W M
C N B S N R E T N A L M S E I
H D O T D R G E E A W T E P G
I R D W Y E K A S R O H H H H
E A N E I A L T V O A A O B T
F W U T P N S L D E R Z E M H
S K O S H E G E I I S T A C E
R C R D I I V F S F R T I N R
E A G R S I N E E A L H B L E
C B P E E X E G Y L W U U O F
I Y E C S S V E S G L W F S O
F K E A E A D S E H C R O T R
F R D H H Y X D L U O H S P E
O U L R T I A N S W E R E D M
J H A V I N G T H E I R D T O
S A I D C G E N O N E K Q H C
```

Hidden Title: _ _ _ _ _ _ _ _

30

Scripture Reference: Acts 10:1-8

Words:

CERTAIN	CAESAREA	CALLED
CORNELIUS	CENTURION	ITALIAN
DEVOUT	FEARED	HOUSE
PEOPLE	VISION	EVIDENTLY
NINTH	ANGEL	COMING
SAYING	LOOKED	AFRAID
PRAYERS	MEMORIAL	JOPPA
SIMON	SURNAME	PETER
LODGETH	TANNER	SPAKE
DEPARTED	HOUSEHOLD	SERVANTS
SOLDIER	WAITED	CONTINUALLY
DECLARED		

Word Search:

```
T H E G D E T R A P E D O S P
C P E T E R E V I D E N T L Y
P O R E I D L O S E S L D E C
R N N L D E F G O V I O I R E
A I G T G E N E N O M O A D N
Y A N N I I C I H U O K R E T
E T A O M N T L C T N E F R U
R R C O I A U O A T E D A A R
S E C A L S R A D R I G E E I
L C W I L N I S L L E R D F O
E A A A E L T V O L A D S O N
A N I L I N E T H S Y T Z R L
V P I R A T A D E G N I Y A S
X U P V O N E A S H O U S E Y
S E R O N M C D U H T N I N D
Y E S E J R E R O E K A P S S
S U R N A M E M H P E O P L E
```

Hidden Title: _ _ _   _ _ _ _ _ _   _ _ _   _ _ _ _ _ _ _ _

31

Scripture Reference: 1 Corinthians 13:1-7

Words:

THOUGH	SPEAK	TONGUES
ANGELS	CHARITY	SOUNDING
BRASS	TINKLING	CYMBAL
PROPHECY	UNDERSTAND	MYSTERIES
KNOWLEDGE	FAITH	REMOVE
MOUNTAINS	NOTHING	BESTOW
GOODS	BURNED	PROFITETH
SUFFERETH	ENVIETH	VAUNTETH
ITSELF	PUFFED	BEHAVE
UNSEEMLY	SEEKETH	EASILY
PROVOKED	THINKETH	REJOICETH
INIQUITY	TRUTH	BEARETH

Word Search:

```
O F H G I S F C R K B H S D O O G
F T S T P A H L N E T R P I D K N
S X M E E A I O E E M R A N W A I
D E A Y R C W G K S O O A S G R D
E K U I S L I N N P T T V N S M N
K N T G E T I O H I S I I E W O U
O Y V D N H E E J R L H M O V U O
V S G I T O C R E E T K T Y A N S
O E V T E Y T D I O R S N L U T L
R E P R N T N B N E E A N I N A E
P K O U W U H U V B S L I S T I G
B E H T E R E F F U S T M A E N N
U T V H U N S E E M L Y H E T S A
R H P R O F I T E T H T Z O H Z J
N D Y T I U Q I N I I B L B U C O
E P U F F E D M L A B M Y C M G F
D E V A H E B E F Z B E A R E T H
```

Hidden Title: _ _ _ _ _ _ _

32

Scripture Reference: 1 Corinthians 13:8-13

Words:

CHARITY	NEVER	FAILETH
WHETHER	THERE	PROPHECIES
THEY	SHALL	FAIL
TONGUES	CEASE	KNOWLEDGE
VANISH	PART	PROPHESY
PERFECT	COME	SPAKE
UNDERSTOOD	THOUGHT	BECAME
CHILDISH	THROUGH	GLASS
DARKLY	FACE	EVEN
KNOWN	ABIDETH	FAITH
HOPE	THESE	THREE
GREATEST		

Word Search:

```
F A C E F S D A T N D E F T D
E L B A O A E H V O Y M A H N
E R I I R P R I O E E A I O E
G L E K D O R T C E H C L U V
D C L H U E S O S E T E E G E
E Y N G T R T A P E H B T H R
L D H M E C E H G H U P H T W
W G V D E C J R X T E G O R T
O L N F W H E T H E R S N R L
N U R S H A L L D O T A Y O P
K E T E T S S A L G L B P Z T
P M M E M P P H S I D L I H C
V O S Y T I R A H C N W O N K
C T F F A I T H K V A N I S H
E P O H H T H E S E E R H T R
```

Hidden Title: _ _ _ _ _ _ _

33

Scripture Reference: Galatians 5:22-26

Words:

FRUIT	SPIRIT	LOVE
JOY	PEACE	SUFFERING
GENTLENESS	GOODNESS	FAITH
MEEKNESS	TEMPERANCE	AGAINST
SUCH	THERE	LAW
CHRIST	HAVE	CRUCIFIED
FLESH	AFFECTIONS	LUSTS
LIVE	WALK	DESIROUS
VAINGLORY	PROVOKING	ONE
ANOTHER	ENVYING	

Word Search:

```
L W F S E N V Y I N G I F
E A R P N S S E N D O O G
G L U E I O C H R I S T D
N K I A M N I T S G H E R
I V T C E E S T E E S P E
K E A E E I R N C I L C H
O V Y I K T T S R E N F T
V O O I N L S O P A F H O
O L J H E G U N R I E F N
R T A N S S L E I R R K A
P V E E S H P O E A L I M
E S V T T M H A R O G A T
S I S I E H C U S Y E A W
L U A T S U F F E R I N G
L F R D E I F I C U R C O
```

Hidden Title: _ _ _ _   _ _   _ _ _   _ _ _ _ _ _

34

Scripture Reference: Ephesians 6:10-17

Words:

FINALLY	BRETHREN	STRONG
WRESTLE	PRINCIPALITIES	POWERS
RULERS	DARKNESS	SPIRITUAL
WICKEDNESS	PLACES	WHEREFORE
WITHSTAND	HAVING	THEREFORE
BREASTPLATE	RIGHTEOUSNESS	PREPARATION
GOSPEL	TAKING	SHIELD
QUENCH	WICKED	HELMET
SALVATION	SPIRIT	

Word Search:

```
S  P  S  E  R  O  F  E  R  E  H  W  R  D  E
E  S  P  P  A  E  R  P  T  R  E  F  P  L  S
T  O  E  R  I  U  L  H  L  S  P  R  W  E  I
A  R  I  N  L  R  E  T  T  A  E  U  I  I  A
L  L  B  E  S  R  I  Y  S  P  C  T  T  H  S
P  G  R  R  E  U  L  T  A  E  I  E  H  S  S
T  S  N  F  E  L  O  R  U  L  R  G  S  S  E
S  B  O  I  A  T  A  E  A  A  N  W  T  A  N
A  R  A  N  V  T  H  P  T  I  L  T  A  L  K
E  T  I  L  I  A  I  R  K  H  E  S  N  V  R
R  F  A  O  I  C  H  A  E  V  G  K  D  A  A
B  R  N  M  N  S  T  R  O  N  G  I  Z  T  D
A  S  W  I  C  K  E  D  N  E  S  S  R  I  J
Z  S  R  E  W  O  P  H  C  N  E  U  Q  O  X
F  P  T  E  M  L  E  H  A  V  P  K  L  N  E
G  O  S  P  E  L  S  P  I  R  I  T  C  J  X
```

Hidden Title: _ _ _ _ _ _ _   _ _ _   _ _ _ _ _ _ _ _ _   _ _ _ _ _ _ _

35

Scripture Reference: Philippians 4:6-13

Words:

CAREFUL	NOTHING	PRAYER
SUPPLICATION	THANKSGIVING	REQUESTS
UNDERSTANDING	HEARTS	CHRIST
FINALLY	BRETHREN	WHATSOEVER
THINGS	HONEST	LOVELY
REPORT	VIRTUE	PRAISE
LEARNED	RECEIVED	REJOICED
GREATLY	FLOURISHED	LACKED
OPPORTUNITY	RESPECT	CONTENT
INSTRUCTED	HUNGRY	SUFFER

Word Search:

```
C H R I S T A H Y R E Q U E S T S
V I R T U E O L T Y M I N R N D H
L F E S I A R P I P O I U E T Q O
D E T C U R T S N I H N T F R G N
L E A R N E D T U Z D N H F O E E
R M S U H L K B T E O S A U P D S
B E E U A R R S R C W J N S E J T
D P V C P E E S O N A P K H R O S
D E K E T P T S P X B W S L E P T
F E V H O A L G P L F I G U J R R
D I R I N S N I O E R P I F O A A
A E N D E I T V C U C O V E I Y E
N R I A H C E A O A E T I R C E H
M N N T L L E L H V T M N A E R C
G L O L Y L F R H W V I G C D S Y
J N G H C B Y R G N U H O X B Z K
I O Y L T A E R G D I S G N I H T
```

Hidden Title: _ _ _ _ _ _ _ _ _

36

Scripture Reference: 1 Thessalonians 5:16-22

Words:

REJOICE	EVERMORE	PRAY
WITHOUT	CEASING	EVERY
THING	GIVE	THANKS
THIS	WILL	GOD
CHRIST	JESUS	CONCERNING
YOU	QUENCH	NOT
SPIRIT	DESPISE	PROVE
ALL	THINGS	HOLD
FAST	GOOD	ABSTAIN
FROM	APPEARANCE	EVIL

Word Search:

```
G T H I N G S T P K E S E
E N O T D E H R E V G Q C
V W I L L A A W O N G U N
E P O N N Y I R I O O E A
R H N K R T P Y O S P N R
Y T S C H E S D A U A C A
F R H O E E C A L S B H E
R T U I H A V N L E S T P
O T H P N T S I O J T I P
M Y O I I G S I G C A R A
N R G T S A F I N Q I I L
P E S I P S E D R G N P I
E V E R M O R E T H O S V
E C I O J E R U O Y C D E
```

Hidden Title: _ _ _ _   _ _   _ _ _ _ _ _ _

77

37

Scripture Reference: 2 Timothy 3:15-17

Words:

FROM	CHILD	THOU
KNOWN	HOLY	SCRIPTURES
WHICH	ARE	ABLE
MAKE	THEE	WISE
UNTO	SALVATION	THROUGH
FAITH	CHRIST	JESUS
ALL	GIVEN	INSPIRATION
GOD	PROFITABLE	FOR
DOCTRINE	REPROOF	CORRECTION
INSTRUCTION	RIGHTEOUSNESS	PERFECT
THOROUGHLY	FURNISHED	GOOD
WORKS		

Word Search:

```
S  C  R  I  P  T  U  R  E  S  F  H  S  N  D
K  T  H  E  E  J  O  T  N  U  G  S  S  O  O
R  E  C  R  F  E  I  P  R  U  E  T  G  I  C
O  U  L  A  R  S  E  N  O  N  I  F  F  T  T
W  T  I  B  A  U  I  R  S  N  W  O  I  C  R
S  T  C  L  A  S  H  U  S  I  R  O  N  E  I
H  A  L  E  H  T  O  P  S  A  Y  R  S  R  N
E  O  L  E  F  E  I  E  F  L  R  P  T  R  E
K  M  D  V  T  R  M  F  O  O  G  E  R  O  O
A  D  C  H  A  O  E  H  O  C  R  R  U  C  J
M  O  G  T  R  T  I  P  C  R  H  F  C  N  L
T  I  I  F  C  H  I  L  D  I  P  R  T  J  E
R  O  Y  L  H  G  U  O  R  O  H  T  I  X  D
N  G  I  V  E  N  W  O  N  K  O  W  O  S  M
B  E  U  P  I  W  U  O  H  T  F  G  N  Z  T
```

Hidden Title: _ _ _ _ _ _ _ _ _ _ _ _ _ _ _ _

38

Scripture Reference: Hebrews 4:11-13

Words:

LABOR	THEREFORE	ENTER
REST	FALL	AFTER
SAME	EXAMPLE	UNBELIEF
WORD	QUICK	POWERFUL
SHARPER	THAN	TWOEDGED
SWORD	PIERCING	EVEN
DIVIDING	ASUNDER	SOUL
SPIRIT	JOINTS	MARROW
DISCERNER	THOUGHTS	INTENTS
HEART	CREATURE	MANIFEST
SIGHT	THINGS	OPENED
EYES		

Word Search:

```
N S J T W O E D G E D H E T
A T S O H S T N E T N I I E
H H M E I I P E R S S R E Q
T G A L S N N I V É I E U D
P U N P I F T G E P T I R R
O O I M G E E S S R C F E O
W H F A H Y E I T K C N A W
E T E X T E A H L S R I R S
R Y S E E S E W S E A T N H
F I T L U R O O C N B M G G
U T L N E R U S E V E N E D
L A D F R L I T D R O W U E
F E O A U D S H A R P E R N
R R M L A B O R R E T N E E
E G N I D I V I D T R Y E P
A Y M H E A R T O E Y C V O
```

Hidden Title: _ _   _ _ _ _   _ _ _ _ _ _ _ _ _ _

39

Scripture Reference: Hebrews 11:1-6

Words:

FAITH	SUBSTANCE	THINGS
HOPED	EVIDENCE	THROUGH
UNDERSTAND	WORLDS	FRAMED
APPEAR	OFFERED	EXCELLENT
SACRIFICE	WITNESS	RIGHTEOUS
GIFTS	BEING	ENOCH
TRANSLATED	SHOULD	DEATH
FOUND	BECAUSE	BEFORE
TESTIMONY	PLEASED	IMPOSSIBLE
BELIEVE	REWARDER	DILIGENTLY

Word Search:

```
E I E X C E L L E N T P O T W
B C M D I L I G E N T L Y H E
R E N P E C N A T S B U S I U
I F L E O D E S A E L P R N O
G A F I D S F R A M E D D G F
H I S A E I S E R O F E B S I
T T T D G V V I H U R G G T E
E H H I L S E E B S N Y X R C
O R F G H R O Q T L N D E A I
U T E O U F O A H O E S R N F
S C U W F O N W M P U S A S I
H L B E A D R I O A H E E L R
D T R E N R T H C T C N P A C
M E A U I S D E T X O T P T A
D L O E E N B E J P N I A E S
T F V T D U G N R Q E W I D N
```

Hidden Title: _ _ _ _ _ _ _ _ _ _ _ _

40

Scripture Reference: Revelation 20:11-15

Words:

GREAT	WHITE	THRONE
FACE	EARTH	HEAVEN
FLED	AWAY	THERE
FOUND	PLACE	THEM
DEAD	SMALL	STAND
BEFORE	BOOKS	WERE
OPENED	ANOTHER	LIFE
JUDGED	THOSE	THINGS
WRITTEN	ACCORDING	THEIR
WORKS	GAVE	DEATH
HELL	DELIVERED	THEY
EVERY	CAST	LAKE
FIRE	THIS	SECOND
WHOSOEVER		

Word Search:

```
T H E I R S T S A C F I R E
S T T C E E K A L O T H I S
T H H C A O I N U S K R O W
A S O E O F H N D G G E T S
N N M B R T D E A D V A T D
D L O A A E R V C E E F O E
G M L E L E E H R R C L T G
Y N D E V L E Y G E A E H D
A E I I H A I T B V L D R U
W X L D V T R F H E P J O J
A E D E R T R E E O U O N Y
D A N F Y O H A R S S P E E
T H I N G S C E E O Q E Q H
N E T T I R W C M H F N A T
A N O T H E R C A W E E I I
E R E W E T I H W X F D B A
```

Hidden Title: _ _ _ _ _ _   _ _   _ _ _ _

Word Search:

	1	2	3	4	5	6	7	8	9	10	11	12	13
1	T	F	T	H	G	I	L	I	M	O	R	F	W
2	N	E	V	A	E	H	R	S	D	I	A	S	A
3	F	D	L	D	T	N	R	S	S	D	A	Y	S
4	I	O	T	A	E	E	O	S	M	O	V	E	D
5	R	G	H	B	T	D	E	P	T	D	T	A	W
6	S	T	Y	A	E	N	I	H	U	E	U	O	E
7	T	D	W	C	K	G	G	V	A	F	O	M	R
8	A	A	E	R	C	I	I	R	I	M	H	R	E
9	S	N	A	E	N	T	T	N	O	D	T	O	D
10	T	D	D	A	P	H	I	R	N	R	I	F	E
11	H	E	A	T	E	T	N	R	F	I	W	I	L
12	E	E	V	E	N	I	N	G	I	A	N	O	L
13	R	N	H	D	N	V	O	I	D	P	C	G	A
14	E	S	L	G	O	O	D	R	H	G	S	E	C

Hidden Title: _ _ _ _ _   _ _ _   _ _   _ _ _ _ _ _ _ _

To read answers to puzzle 1, see clues on page 87. For example: The (9,7): Look down to the ninth column and across to the seventh to find the first letter, **T**, of the word **The**. All the remaining answers can be interpreted the same way.

1

THE (9,7)	BEGINNING (5,4)
GOD (5,2)	CREATED (7,4)
HEAVEN (2,6)	AND (8,1)
EARTH (6,10)	WAS (1,13)
WITHOUT (11,11)	FORM (10,12)
VOID (13,6)	DARKNESS (10,2)
UPON (6,9)	FACE (11,9)
DEEP (7,2)	SPIRIT (14,11)
MOVED (4,9)	WATERS (7,3)
SAID (2,12)	LET (3,3)
THERE (10,1)	LIGHT (1,7)
SAW (9,1)	THAT (6,2)
GOOD (14,4)	DIVIDED (9,10)
FROM (1,12)	CALLED (14,13)
DAY (3,10)	NIGHT (9,5)
EVENING (12,2)	MORNING (8,10)
WERE (5,13)	FIRST (3,1)

Hidden Title: First Day of Creation

2

SAID (7,2)	MAKE (15,5)
IMAGE (14,9)	LIKENESS (11,11)
HAVE (1,8)	DOMINION (13,12)
FISH (1,9)	FOWL (2,12)
CATTLE (6,15)	EARTH (12,7)
CREEPING (11,2)	THING (1,15)
CREATED (16,8)	MALE (14,15)
FEMALE (4,11)	BLESSED (9,2)
FRUITFUL (4,14)	MULTIPLY (15,6)
REPLENISH (4,13)	SUBDUE (14,6)
LIVING (1,5)	MOVETH (11,1)
BEHOLD (17,14)	GIVEN (3,14)
HERB (6,1)	BEARING (13,9)
SEED (17,1)	TREE (12,3)
YIELDING (7,1)	SHALL (6,5)
MEAT (6,8)	BEAST (1,3)
WHEREIN (13,13)	THERE (1,15)
LIFE (12,4)	GREEN (5,11)
MADE (14,10)	VERY (17,8)
GOOD (17,9)	EVENING (5,3)
MORNING (13,2)	SIXTH (16,9)

Hidden Title: God Makes Man

3

SERPENT (11,1)	BECAUSE (16,7)
CURSED (11,9)	ABOVE (1,12)
CATTLE (15,8)	EVERY (12,1)
BEAST (1,11)	FIELD (8,3)
BELLY (17,6)	SHALL (14,7)
ENMITY (17,12)	BETWEEN (13,13)
WOMAN (2,2)	BRUISE (6,14)
GREATLY (16,1)	MULTIPLY (9,6)
SORROW (5,15)	CONCEPTION
BRING (5,14)	(10,11)
CHILDREN (11,9)	FORTH (9,1)
HUSBAND (9,13)	DESIRE (16,14)
VOICE (2,5)	HEARKENED (1,13)
WHICH (5,11)	EATEN (10,5)
SAYING (6,9)	COMMANDED (4,3)
THORNS (12,6)	GROUND (13,12)
SWEAT (5,15)	THISTLES (11,12)
RETURN (7,9)	BREAD (13,1)
CALLED (1,3)	TAKEN (17,15)
LIVING (6,1)	MOTHER (11,15)

Hidden Title: Adam and Eve Disobey

4

PLACE (6,11)	WHICH (2,3)
ABRAHAM (14,12)	BUILT (2,9)
ALTAR (9,2)	THERE (6,5)
ORDER (8,10)	BOUND (16,2)
ISAAC (7,1)	STRETCHED
FORTH (8,4)	(13,11)
ANGEL (4,2)	KNIFE (2,17)
HEAVEN (15,14)	CALLED (15,17)
SEEING (3,17)	FEAREST (13,10)
LIFTED (12,5)	WITHHELD (1,14)
BEHIND (7,7)	LOOKED (1,7)
THICKET (15,5)	CAUGHT (10,1)
BURNT (1,8)	HORNS (2,4)
STEAD (5,12)	OFFERING (16,3)
MOUNT (1,6)	JEHOVAH (9,4)
SWORN (9,16)	MYSELF (17,15)
MULTIPLY (14,3)	BLESSING (7,7)
SEASHORE (9,15)	STARS (6,15)
ENEMIES (15,16)	POSSESS (1,15)
EARTH (10,4)	NATIONS (17,1)
OBEYED (4,16)	BLESSED (16,14)
VOICE (12,11)	

Hidden Title: Test of Faith

5

BONDAGE (15,9)
GRAVEN (10,6)
HEAVEN (11,11)
JEALOUS (2,17)
INIQUITY (3,9)
CHILDREN (8,1)
GENERATION (13,7)
THOUSANDS (1,9)
GUILTLESS (6,15)
REMEMBER (4,5)
SEVENTH (12,7)
MANSERVANT
  (5,13)
STRANGER (9,7)
WHEREFORE
  (14,13)
HALLOWED (18,14)
MOTHER (17,7)
COMMIT (18,1)
WITNESS (7,1)

BEFORE (14,17)
LIKENESS (2,13)
THYSELF (11,3)
VISITING (13,16)
FATHERS (13,14)
FOURTH (16,11)
SHOWING (2,7)
COMMANDMENTS
  (13,12)
TAKETH (16,1)
SABBATH (3,7)
DAUGHTER (8,18)
CATTLE (17,18)
RESTED (17,1)
BLESSED (15,2)
FATHER (14,8)
GIVETH (3,16)
ADULTERY (8,11)
AGAINST (9,18)
NEIGHBOR (5,2)

Hidden Title: Ten Laws from God

6

BLESSED (13,8)
COUNSEL (2,11)
STANDETH (9,10)
SITTETH (1,8)
SCORNFUL (14,13)
LORD (11,13)
NIGHT (5,6)
LIKE (16,11)
PLANTED (16,2)
WATER (1,1)
FORTH (17,7)
SEASON (15,16)
WITHER (1,1)
PROSPER (6,2)
WIND (2,7)
AWAY (1,2)
STAND (9,10)
CONGREGATION
  (14,3)
KNOWETH (16,4)

WALKETH (7,13)
UNGODLY (6,4)
SINNERS (8,3)
SEAT (14,15)
DELIGHT (15,10)
MEDITATE (13,16)
SHALL (1,15)
TREE (4,16)
RIVERS (14,10)
BRINGETH (7,1)
FRUIT (13,3)
LEAF (17,10)
WHATSOEVER
  (11,15)
CHAFF (9,14)
DRIVETH (14,1)
THEREFORE (7,7)
JUDGMENT (3,5)
RIGHTEOUS (2,15)
PERISH (2,13)

Hidden Title: Happy in Doing Right

7

EXCELLENT (11,9)
GLORY (15,6)
MOUTH (9,11)
SUCKLINGS (4,11)
STRENGTH (5,15)
THINE (16,6)
STILL (14,16)
AVENGER (6,16)
FINGERS (13,13)
MINDFUL (3,15)
LITTLE (12,1)
ANGELS (2,4)
HONOR (6,14)
WORKS (5,16)
THINGS (16,14)
BEASTS (8,12)
WHATSOEVER
  (12,7)
THROUGH (14,5)

EARTH (10,7)
HEAVENS (7,1)
BABES (16,2)
ORDAINED (1,8)
BECAUSE (3,3)
MIGHTEST (13,10)
ENEMY (13,5)
CONSIDER (2,12)
STARS (5,2)
VISITEST (12,8)
LOWER (5,9)
CROWNED (8,1)
DOMINION (3,8)
HANDS (15,1)
SHEEP (15,15)
FIELD (2,15)
PASSETH (13,9)
PATHS (16,16)

Hidden Title: Glory of God

8

SHEPHERD (4,8)
MAKETH (15,12)
PASTURES (12,13)
BESIDE (11,1)
WATERS (7,3)
PATHS (12,13)
THOUGH (15,2)
VALLEY (16,9)
DEATH (5,7)
COMFORT (16,15)
TABLE (1,14)
PRESENCE (12,14)
ANOINTEST (6,5)
SURELY (7,4)
MERCY (6,2)
DWELL (2,8)
HOUSE (16,10)

SHALL (12,5)
GREEN (12,8)
LEADETH (6,1)
STILL (14,14)
RESTORETH (7,15)
RIGHTEOUSNESS
  (13,1)
THROUGH (6,10)
SHADOW (1,15)
STAFF (5,8)
PREPAREST (2,13)
BEFORE (6,12)
ENEMIES (7,12)
RUNNETH (14,1)
GOODNESS (13,4)
FOLLOW (1,7)

Hidden Title: A Song of David

9

UNTO (14,10)
LORD (12,2)
SOUL (14,12)
ASHAMED (1,12)
TRIUMPH (8,9)
NONE (12,11)
WAIT (7,10)
WHICH (10,2)
WITHOUT (1,13)
SHOW (11,4)
TEACH (13,10)
REMEMBER (2,8)
MERCIES (15,9)
KINDNESSES
  (11,11)
HAVE (1,7)
EVER (5,8)
YOUTH (8,6)
ACCORDING (9,4)

THEE (7,1)
LIFT (2,6)
TRUST (7,9)
ENEMIES (6,11)
OVER (5,7)
THAT (4,5)
THEM (14,14)
TRANSGRESS
  (10,1)
CAUSE (1,1)
WAYS (15,5)
PATHS (8,5)
TENDER (9,14)
LOVING (15,4)
THEY (15,10)
BEEN (10,14)
SINS (11,10)
TRANSGRESSIONS
  (15,14)

Hidden Title: Trust in the Lord

10

THESE (6,1)
DOTH (7,1)
HATE (2,13)
ABOMINATION
  (13,12)
PROUD (7,11)
LYING (8,11)
HANDS (9,6)
SHED (15,2)
BLOOD (11,9)
DEVISETH (9,13)
IMAGINATIONS
  (12,2)
SWIFT (10,13)
MISCHIEF (2,11)
WITNESS (10,12)
LIES (1,5)
BRETHREN (7,14)

THINGS (8,1)
LORD (1,12)
SEVEN (4,6)
UNTO (2,14)
LOOK (13,7)
TONGUE (6,1)
THAT (14,4)
INNOCENT (4,5)
HEART (13,2)
WICKED (9,3)
FEET (13,13)
RUNNING (12,3)
FALSE (15,12)
SPEAKETH (14,10)
SOWETH (5,11)
AMONG (11,2)
DISCORD (3,3)

Hidden Title: Seven Things God Hates

11

RETURNED (9,12)
THAT (2,11)
SWIFT (6,8)
STRONG (1,1)
BREAD (1,13)
RICHES (4,1)
FAVOR (7,10)
TIME (9,3)
HAPPENETH (12,3)
ALSO (12,13)
FISHES (1,7)
EVIL (14,3)
CAUGHT (5,2)
SNARED (3,8)
FALLETH (13,13)
UPON (15,13)

UNDER (6,3)
RACE (8,11)
BATTLE (15,9)
NEITHER (12,11)
WISE (14,10)
UNDERSTANDING
  (15,13)
SKILL (6,8)
CHANCE (11,2)
THEM (13,6)
KNOWETH (13,1)
TAKEN (5,9)
BIRDS (7,3)
SONS (9,1)
WHEN (14,10)
SUDDENLY (4,4)

Hidden Title: Success and Failure

12

REJOICE (11,6)
HEART (1,11)
DAYS (4,1)
WAYS (16,11)
SIGHT (5,7)
KNOW (2,7)
THINGS (3,8)
JUDGMENT (6,12)
REMOVE (12,14)
AWAY (16,4)
FLESH (4,2)
VANITY (1,1)
CREATOR (14,7)
YEARS (14,13)
NIGH (5,14)
PLEASURE (8,5)
MOON (9,9)
DARKENED (10,13)
RETURN (12,7)

YOUTH (12,1)
CHEER (12,10)
WALK (8,11)
THINE (1,13)
EYES (1,5)
THESE (16,5)
BRING (13,5)
THEREFORE (1,14)
SORROW (6,14)
EVIL (8,1)
CHILDHOOD (7,1)
REMEMBER (12,8)
COME (11,11)
DRAW (11,5)
HAVE (5,3)
LIGHT (13,8)
STARS (15,1)
CLOUDS (6,1)
RAIN (2,11)

Hidden Title: How the Young Should Live

13

SHALL (10,5)
BEFORE (8,1)
PLANT (13,8)
GROUND (8,3)
FORM (8,9)
WHEN (4,12)
BEAUTY (4,11)
SHOULD (2,4)
DESPISED (8,8)
SORROWS (12,12)
WITH (2,7)
WERE (6,2)
FROM (2,5)

GROW (11,8)
TENDER (9,6)
ROOT (1,6)
HATH (13,1)
COMELINESS
  (3,10)
THERE (5,9)
THAT (6,9)
DESIRE (7,1)
REJECTED (12,4)
ACQUAINTED (4,10)
GRIEF (14,10)
FACES (14,6)
ESTEEMED (6,4)

Hidden Title: Suffering and Glory

15

THEN (16,6)
GALILEE (8,9)
JOHN (2,1)
FORBADE (5,12)
HAVE (9,4)
ANSWERING
  (13,11)
BECOMETH (9,1)
RIGHTEOUSNESS
  (2,13)
WHEN (7,1)
STRAIGHTWAY
  (11,11)
HEAVENS (12,8)
SPIRIT (4,2)
LIKE (11,13)
LIGHTING (12,5)
HEAVEN (6,10)
WHOM (1,9)
PLEASED (2,4)

JESUS (15,1)
JORDAN (10,13)
BAPTIZED (8,3)
SAYING (13,12)
NEED (6,1)
SAID (14,12)
FULFIL (15,9)
WENT (13,1)
SUFFERED (14,12)
WATER (16,5)
OPENED (8,1)
DESCENDING
  (2,14)
DOVE (11,5)
VOICE (16,9)
BELOVED (8,5)
WELL (1,9)

Hidden Title: Jesus Is Baptized

14

NEBUCHADNEZZAR
  (14,15)
AGAINST (2,14)
MESHACH (5,7)
THEREFORE (8,12)
COMMANDED
  (9,15)
FURNACE (3,5)
TIMES (12,1)
MIGHTY (5,9)
FIERY (7,1)
THEIR (4,2)
GARMENTS (5,14)
BECAUSE (12,13)
URGENT (17,8)
FLAME (13,9)
ASTONISHED
  (15,16)
COUNSELORS (8,1)
LOOSE (17,13)
FOURTH (4,7)

CHANGED (15,9)
SHADRACH (16,13)
ABEDNEGO (1,1)
SPAKE (12,12)
SHOULD (2,1)
SEVEN (10,7)
HEATED (3,15)
BURNING (14,9)
BOUND (7,9)
COATS (16,1)
MIDST (14,14)
COMMANDMENT
  (17,1)
EXCEEDING (1,7)
THREE (2,8)
HASTE (1,3)
ANSWERED (17,2)
WALKING (7,10)

Hidden Title: Four Men in the Furnace

16

MULTITUDES
  (10,15)
DISCIPLES (2,3)
MOUTH (10,12)
BLESSED (2,5)
SPIRIT (1,7)
HEAVEN (7,6)
COMFORTED (1,16)
INHERIT (7,3)
HUNGER (6,12)
RIGHTEOUSNESS
  (13,3)
MERCIFUL (16,16)
PURE (9,3)
PEACEMAKERS
  (15,12)
PERSECUTED
  (7,11)
MANNER (4,13)
AGAINST (12,2)
REJOICE (14,10)
GREAT (16,1)

MOUNTAIN (11,16)
OPENED (14,6)
TAUGHT (5,14)
POOR (15,16)
KINGDOM (5,1)
MOURN (16,7)
MEEK (4,11)
EARTH (14,1)
THIRST (10,3)
FILLED (15,7)
OBTAIN (13,11)
HEART (1,1)
CHILDREN
  (12,9)
REVILE (1,11)
EVIL (2,10)
FALSELY (16,11)
EXCEEDING (2,12)
REWARD (1,6)

Hidden Title: Beatitudes

17

PRAYEST (17,8)
STANDING (8,1)
CORNERS (16,15)
VERILY (4,14)
REWARD (2,9)
CLOSET (2,8)
SECRET (4,15)
REPETITIONS (11,15)
THINK (17,1)
SPEAKING (13,1)
THINGS (5,16)
HEAVEN (12,14)
KINGDOM (12,1)
DAILY (17,14)
FORGIVE (7,2)
TEMPTATION (8,16)
POWER (17,8)
HEAVENLY (12,14)

HYPOCRITES (4,4)
SYNAGOGUES (1,12)
STREETS (14,2)
THEIR (5,4)
ENTER (13,12)
FATHER (13,9)
OPENLY (11,6)
HEATHEN (16,7)
HEARD (2,16)
KNOWETH (7,5)
MANNER (1,9)
HALLOWED (15,11)
EARTH (16,11)
BREAD (10,13)
DEBTORS (2,3)
DELIVER (9,6)
GLORY (1,3)
TRESPASSES (10,7)

Hidden Title: Prayer for Believers

18

SPAKE (2,2)
PARABLES (6,8)
BEHOLD (10,11)
WENT (15,11)
SEEDS (15,5)
WAYSIDE (1,13)
CAME (16,15)
STONY (12,6)
WHERE (5,15)
MUCH (6,12)
FORTHWITH (16,1)
BECAUSE (14,14)
SCORCHED (14,10)
WITHERED (11,1)
CHOKED (4,6)
GROUND (1,14)
FRUIT (3,7)
SIXTYFOLD (2,1)

MANY (12,8)
SAYING (2,12)
SOWER (12,15)
FORTH (7,1)
FELL (1,4)
FOWLS (8,1)
DEVOURED (9,13)
PLACES (7,11)
THEY (1,15)
EARTH (1,5)
SPRUNG (13,1)
DEEPNESS (12,4)
ROOT (15,7)
THORNS (8,11)
GOOD (4,11)
BROUGHT (7,2)
HUNDREDFOLD (4,1)
THIRTYFOLD (16,12)

Hidden Title: Parable of the Soils

19

ORDAINED (2,11)
SEND (16,2)
FORTH (15,13)
POWER (13,11)
SICKNESSES (12,2)
DEVILS (8,1)
SURNAMED (2,3)
JAMES (9,12)
JOHN (16,10)
BOANERGES (7,14)
THUNDER (9,13)
PHILIP (7,1)
MATTHEW (10,1)
ALPHEUS (14,2)
CANAANITE (1,9)
ISCARIOT (14,13)

TWELVE (11,8)
THEM (4,11)
PREACH (15,2)
HEAL (11,2)
CAST (16,9)
SIMON (10,10)
PETER (1,14)
ZEBEDEE (3,9)
BROTHER (8,3)
SONS (9,11)
ANDREW (14,4)
BARTHOLOMEW (13,12)
THOMAS (4,11)
THADDEUS (8,12)
JUDAS (12,8)
BETRAYED (4,2)

Hidden Title: Jesus Appoints Apostles

20

THERE (8,10)
SAME (8,3)
SHEPHERDS (14,3)
FIELD (15,13)
WATCH (1,9)
THEIR (6,6)
NIGHT (7,15)
LORD (12,13)
UPON (1,13)
GLORY (2,7)
ROUND (9,5)
THEY (15,2)
AFRAID (16,14)
UNTO (4,15)
BEHOLD (1,8)
TIDINGS (10,11)
WHICH (1,14)
PEOPLE (16,3)
THIS (8,7)
DAVID (1,1)
CHRIST (10,13)

WERE (7,2)
COUNTRY (11,9)
ABIDING (9,3)
KEEPING (3,1)
OVER (12,2)
FLOCK (10,15)
ANGEL (13,2)
CAME (14,6)
THEM (2,15)
SHONE (16,1)
ABOUT (12,12)
SORE (10,3)
SAID (1,2)
FEAR (2,3)
GOOD (11,1)
GREAT (9,10)
SHALL (4,11)
BORN (4,13)
CITY (6,12)
SAVIOUR (16,7)

Hidden Title: Shepherds Hear About Jesus

21

RETURNED (15,14)
SPIRIT (6,11)
TEMPTED (12,14)
AFTERWARD (3,6)
COMMAND (1,13)
SAYING (11,7)
TAKING (15,6)
SHOWED (6,2)
MOMENT (8,15)
WORSHIP (8,7)
BROUGHT (1,15)
PINNACLE (12,6)
ANGELS (14,8)
TEMPTATION
  (10,11)
SEASON (6,2)

JORDAN (14,2)
WILDERNESS
  (3,11)
NOTHING (7,1)
HUNGERED (14,9)
ANSWERED (16,1)
WRITTEN (1,14)
MOUNTAIN (1,11)
KINGDOMS (8,12)
DELIVERED (10,16)
BEHIND (7,6)
JERUSALEM (9,1)
TEMPLE (16,2)
CHARGE (16,8)
DEPARTED (13,13)

Hidden Title: Satan Tempts Jesus

22

CERTAIN (5,7)
TEMPTED (16,7)
MASTER (9,7)
ETERNAL (14,6)
ANSWERING (13,5)
WILLING (14,13)
HIMSELF (11,3)
JERICHO (7,6)
STRIPPED (16,15)
WOUNDED (7,4)
LEAVING (1,14)
PASSED (15,2)
LOOKED (17,12)
JOURNEYED (4,14)
WOUNDS (14,1)
BROUGHT (16,1)

LAWYER (14,11)
SAYING (1,2)
INHERIT (8,1)
WRITTEN (3,6)
NEIGHBOR (12,15)
JUSTIFY (1,15)
JERUSALEM (1,15)
THIEVES (1,6)
RAIMENT (1,3)
DEPARTED (13,2)
PRIEST (8,15)
LEVITE (17,1)
SAMARITAN (11,5)
COMPASSION (5,6)
POURING (15,14)
SHOWED (12,12)

Hidden Title: Who Is My Neighbor

23

YOUNGER (7,15)
GOODS (11,9)
LIVING (10,16)
JOURNEY (13,9)
WASTED (14,13)
RIOTOUS (4,10)
JOINED (14,3)
CITIZEN (2,5)
SWINE (15,1)
BELLY (2,10)
HIRED (7,9)
BREAD (8,2)
SPARE (5,10)
HUNGER (10,10)
SINNED (7,14)
WORTHY (16,13)
COMPASSION
  (14,4)
BRING (1,16)
FATTED (1,3)
ALIVE (9,2)

PORTION (4,8)
DIVIDED (6,7)
GATHERED (9,12)
COUNTRY (1,15)
SUBSTANCE
  (15,16)
FAMINE (12,8)
HIMSELF (1,7)
FIELDS (2,1)
FILLED (5,7)
HUSKS (3,7)
SERVANTS (14,1)
ENOUGH (15,6)
PERISH (12,14)
ARISE (11,4)
HEAVEN (16,11)
CALLED (1,2)
KISSED (11,2)
SHOES (15,16)
MERRY (14,9)
FOUND (16,1)

Hidden Title: A Lost Son

24

PLACE (8,5)
CALVARY (1,7)
MALEFACTORS
  (14,2)
HAND (5,8)
THEN (10,8)
JESUS (16,1)
FORGIVE (17,7)
KNOW (6,1)
PARTED (1,8)
CAST (6,13)
PEOPLE (5,12)
BEHOLDING (3,3)
DERIDED (16,8)
SAVED (17,5)
HIMSELF (5,7)
SOLDIERS (11,15)
OFFERING (4,5)
KING (6,11)
OVER (15,10)
LATIN (1,16)

CALLED (17,13)
CRUCIFIED (3,13)
RIGHT (12,5)
LEFT (15,1)
SAID (2,8)
FATHER (11,14)
THEM (4,4)
WHAT (13,4)
RAIMENT (11,6)
LOTS (2,15)
STOOD (13,12)
RULERS (16,10)
SAYING (4,6)
OTHERS (1,14)
CHRIST (2,7)
MOCKED (8,16)
VINEGAR (15,12)
JEWS (14,15)
WRITTEN (10,4)
LETTERS (9,9)
HEBREW (15,5)

Hidden Title: Prince of Life Is Killed

25

FIRST (6,13)
MORNING (8,14)
BRINGING (14,7)
PREPARED (1,11)
OTHERS (1,3)
STONE (2,1)
ENTERED (11,10)
PERPLEXED (3,4)
BEHOLD (9,1)
SHINING (10,7)
AFRAID (13,2)
THEIR (2,8)
EARTH (10,1)
RISEN (10,13)
GALILEE (2,10)
DELIVERED (14,6)
SINFUL (15,15)
THIRD (8,4)
WORDS (13,8)

EARLY (1,16)
SEPULCHRE
(15,15)
SPICES (16,8)
CERTAIN (14,16)
FOUND (3,12)
ROLLED (14,8)
JESUS (4,10)
THEREABOUT
(6,10)
STOOD (15,4)
GARMENTS (11,7)
BOWED (5,2)
FACES (3,12)
LIVING (15,10)
SPAKE (10,7)
SAYING (16,15)
HANDS (12,6)
CRUCIFIED (9,12)
REMEMBERED
(3,3)
RETURNED (1,6)

Hidden Title: Jesus Lives

26

LOVED (2,6)
GAVE (10,4)
BEGOTTEN (7,15)
BELIEVETH (1,10)
PERISH (7,14)
EVERLASTING
(14,1)
SENT (1,3)
MIGHT (5,11)
ALREADY (13,1)
BELIEVED (8,12)
THIS (4,3)
LIGHT (15,8)
RATHER (5,1)
THEIR (16,5)
EVIL (4,12)
HATETH (6,1)
REPROVED (13,3)
MADE (16,6)

WORLD (8,5)
ONLY (13,11)
WHOSOEVER (4,4)
SHOULD (15,6)
HAVE (2,15)
LIFE (1,4)
THROUGH (1,8)
SAVED (6,11)
BECAUSE (2,13)
NAME (8,14)
CONDEMNATION
(14,12)
DARKNESS (12,14)
THAN (16,10)
DEEDS (14,9)
EVERY (11,7)
NEITHER (14,2)
TRUTH (15,15)
MANIFEST (11,13)

Hidden Title: God Loves All People

27

TIBERIAS (10,14)
FOLLOWED (15,8)
DISEASED (1,8)
DISCIPLES (9,8)
COMPANY (11,13)
ANSWERED (8,14)
PENNYWORTH
(17,12)
ANDREW (17,14)
BARLEY (16,14)
FISHES (6,6)
THOUSAND (9,15)
DISTRIBUTED
(11,5)
GATHER (17,11)
GATHERED (7,4)
BASKETS (11,16)

MULTITUDE (4,9)
MIRACLES (14,1)
MOUNTAIN (16,12)
PASSOVER (8,2)
PHILIP (6,1)
HUNDRED (7,1)
SUFFICIENT (10,16)
BROTHER (2,13)
LOAVES (1,10)
NUMBER (17,1)
THANKS (13,6)
FILLED (12,15)
FRAGMENTS (2,15)
TWELVE (12,6)
REMAINED (16,3)

Hidden Title: Food for Five Thousand

28

YOUR (12,8)
TROUBLED (2,3)
ALSO (13,4)
HOUSE (10,10)
MANSIONS (1,10)
WOULD (8,14)
TOLD (14,1)
PLACE (4,1)
COME (8,2)
RECEIVE (12,1)
MYSELF (15,14)
WHERE (14,5)
WHITHER (10,2)
THOMAS (11,9)
LORD (1,14)
GOEST (2,1)
TRUTH (7,9)
COMETH (13,8)
SHOULD (1,9)

HEART (9,2)
BELIEVE (9,14)
FATHER (11,7)
MANY (15,9)
WERE (4,11)
HAVE (1,13)
PREPARE (9,7)
WILL (15,4)
AGAIN (12,6)
UNTO (12,13)
THAT (1,7)
THERE (1,12)
KNOW (3,11)
SAID (8,11)
THOU (4,4)
JESUS (15,13)
LIFE (7,6)
KNOWN (2,4)
FROM (15,12)

Hidden Title: Comfort for Believers

JUDAS (15,1)
RECEIVED (13,2)
CHIEF (2,1)
PHARISEES (3,14)
TORCHES (12,14)
JESUS (1,2)
KNOWING (1,1)
SHOULD (13,13)
SAID (16,1)
WHOM (3,11)
THEY (14,5)
NAZARETH (8,14)
BETRAYED (5,14)
BACKWARD (10,2)
GROUND (9,3)
THEIR (15,8)
MIGHT (1,15)
SPAKE (7,4)
LOST (9,14)
Hidden Title: Betrayed

HAVING (15,2)
OFFICERS (14,1)
PRIESTS (10,3)
LANTERNS (2,11)
WEAPONS (1,14)
THEREFORE (5,15)
THINGS (6,4)
COME (16,15)
THEM (5,15)
SEEK (9,5)
ANSWERED (14,7)
WHICH (10,11)
STOOD (2,13)
FELL (8,8)
THESE (14,5)
SAYING (11,6)
FULFILLED (11,13)
GAVEST (3,7)
NONE (16,10)

30

CERTAIN (10,2)
CALLED (8,3)
CENTURION (3,15)
DEVOUT (2,10)
HOUSE (14,10)
VISION (11,8)
NINTH (15,14)
COMING (9,3)
LOOKED (3,12)
PRAYERS (3,1)
JOPPA (16,5)
SURNAME (17,1)
LODGETH (12,15)
SPAKE (16,14)
HOUSEHOLD (17,9)
SOLDIER (3,9)
CONTINUALLY (2,1)

CAESAREA (15,7)
CORNELIUS (7,9)
ITALIAN (6,8)
FEARED (10,14)
PEOPLE (17,10)
EVIDENTLY (2,7)
ANGEL (7,3)
SAYING (13,15)
AFRAID (8,13)
MEMORIAL (17,8)
SIMON (3,11)
PETER (2,2)
TANNER (12,8)
DEPARTED (1,12)
SERVANTS (17,1)
WAITED (10,3)
DECLARED (4,5)
Hidden Title: The Gospel for Gentiles

31

THOUGH (12,12)
TONGUES (9,7)
CHARITY (1,8)
BRASS (1,11)
CYMBAL (16,14)
UNDERSTAND
  (11,6)
KNOWLEDGE (1,10)
REMOVE (1,9)
NOTHING (10,9)
GOODS (1,17)
PROFITETH (14,3)
ENVIETH (5,1)
ITSELF (6,12)
BEHAVE (17,7)
SEEKETH (8,2)
PROVOKED (11,1)
REJOICETH (9,11)
TRUTH (9,4)
Hidden Title: Of Gifts

SPEAK (1,6)
ANGELS (13,17)
SOUNDING (8,17)
TINKLING (11,15)
PROPHECY (2,13)
MYSTERIES (3,3)
FAITH (17,9)
MOUNTAINS (5,16)
BESTOW (11,10)
BURNED (12,1)
SUFFERETH
  (12,11)
VAUNTETH (7,15)
PUFFED (16,2)
UNSEEMLY (13,5)
EASILY (13,14)
THINKETH (8,5)
INIQUITY (15,10)
BEARETH (17,11)

32

CHARITY (13,10)
FAILETH (1,13)
THERE (6,5)
THEY (5,11)
FAIL (1,5)
CEASE (8,6)
VANISH (14,10)
PROPHESY (3,6)
COME (14,1)
UNDERSTOOD
  (10,2)
BECAME (6,12)
THROUGH (1,9)
DARKLY (1,7)
EVEN (5,15)
ABIDETH (1,2)
HOPE (15,4)
THREE (15,14)
Hidden Title: And Love

NEVER (2,15)
WHETHER (9,5)
PROPHECIES
  (10,15)
SHALL (10,4)
TONGUES (11,15)
KNOWLEDGE (11,1)
PART (11,13)
PERFECT (12,1)
SPAKE (11,6)
THOUGHT (1,14)
CHILDISH (12,15)
GLASS (11,10)
FACE (1,1)
KNOWN (13,15)
FAITH (14,4)
THESE (15,6)
GREATEST (7,9)

33

FRUIT (1,3)
LOVE (9,2)
PEACE (2,4)
GENTLENESS (4,10)
FAITH (15,2)
TEMPERANCE (14,4)
SUCH (13,9)
LAW (11,11)
HAVE (9,4)
FLESH (7,12)
LUSTS (15,1)
WALK (1,2)
VAINGLORY (5,2)
ONE (15,13)
ENVYING (1,5)

SPIRIT (7,8)
JOY (9,3)
SUFFERING (14,5)
GOODNESS (2,13)
MEEKNESS (4,5)
AGAINST (13,12)
THERE (7,13)
CHRIST (3,7)
CRUCIFIED (15,12)
AFFECTIONS (10,13)
LIVE (14,1)
DESIROUS (3,13)
PROVOKING (11,1)
ANOTHER (10,13)

Hidden Title: Life in the Spirit

34

FINALLY (11,2)
STRONG (12,6)
PRINCIPALITIES (15,2)
RULERS (2,7)
SPIRITUAL (1,3)
PLACES (2,8)
WITHSTAND (3,13)
THEREFORE (2,9)
RIGHTEOUSNESS (13,13)
GOSPEL (16,1)
SHIELD (6,14)
WICKED (13,3)
SALVATION (7,14)

BRETHREN (5,3)
WRESTLE (8,12)
POWERS (14,7)
DARKNESS (12,15)
WICKEDNESS (13,3)
WHEREFORE (1,12)
HAVING (11,7)
BREASTPLATE (12,1)
PREPARATION (2,13)
TAKING (12,7)
QUENCH (14,13)
HELMET (15,8)
SPIRIT (16,7)

Hidden Title: Prepare for Spiritual Battles

35

CAREFUL (15,14)
PRAYER (9,16)
THANKSGIVING (4,13)
UNDERSTANDING (3,13)
CHRIST (1,1)
BRETHREN (6,8)
THINGS (17,17)
LOVELY (10,10)
VIRTUE (2,1)
LEARNED (5,1)
REJOICED (8,15)
FLOURISHED (15,7)
OPPORTUNITY (11,9)
CONTENT (7,10)
HUNGRY (16,12)

NOTHING (16,2)
SUPPLICATION (6,3)
REQUESTS (1,10)
HEARTS (13,17)
FINALLY (10,1)
WHATSOEVER (15,10)
HONEST (2,17)
REPORT (8,15)
PRAISE (3,8)
RECEIVED (15,8)
GREATLY (17,9)
LACKED (6,6)
RESPECT (7,6)
INSTRUCTED (4,10)
SUFFER (7,14)

Hidden Title: A Holy Mind

36

REJOICE (14,7)
PRAY (1,9)
CEASING (6,4)
THING (6,2)
THANKS (1,8)
WILL (3,2)
CHRIST (14,11)
CONCERNING (10,10)
QUENCH (2,12)
SPIRIT (13,12)
PROPHESYINGS (12,1)
ALL (6,9)
HOLD (5,2)
GOOD (3,11)
FROM (7,1)
EVIL (14,13)

EVERMORE (13,1)
WITHOUT (3,8)
EVERY (2,1)
GIVE (10,9)
THIS (8,2)
GOD (12,10)
JESUS (9,10)
YOU (14,10)
NOT (2,2)
DESPISE (12,8)
PROVE (5,7)
THINGS (1,2)
FAST (11,7)
ABSTAIN (6,11)
APPEARANCE (10,13)

Hidden Title: Keep on Praying

37

FROM (12,4)
THOU (15,10)
HOLY (10,8)
WHICH (14,12)
ABLE (4,4)
THEE (2,2)
UNTO (2,10)
THROUGH (7,6)
CHRIST (10,10)
ALL (5,5)
INSPIRATION (4,11)
PROFITABLE
  (12,11)
DOCTRINE (1,15)
CORRECTION
  (10,14)
RIGHTEOUSNESS
  (13,1)
THOROUGHLY
  (13,12)
GOOD (15,12)

CHILD (12,5)
KNOWN (14,10)
SCRIPTURES (1,1)
ARE (7,10)
MAKE (11,1)
WISE (5,11)
SALVATION (6,1)
FAITH (3,5)
JESUS (2,6)
GIVEN (14,2)
GOD (3,13)
FOR (8,9)
REPROOF (10,12)
INSTRUCTION
  (5,13)
PERFECT (11,8)
FURNISHED (1,11)
WORKS (5,1)

Hidden Title: Scripture from God

39

FAITH (4,2)
THINGS (1,14)
EVIDENCE (8,8)
UNDERSTAND
  (3,15)
FRAMED (5,7)
OFFERED (9,7)
SACRIFICE (15,15)
RIGHTEOUS (3,1)
BEING (12,3)
TRANSLATED (7,14)
DEATH (16,5)
BECAUSE (15,7)
TESTIMONY (16,4)
IMPOSSIBLE (1,2)
REWARDER (9,2)

SUBSTANCE (3,13)
HOPED (13,8)
THROUGH (14,9)
WORLDS (11,8)
APPEAR (15,13)
EXCELLENT (1,3)
WITNESS (16,12)
GIFTS (7,5)
ENOCH (16,11)
SHOULD (8,6)
FOUND (16,2)
BEFORE (6,13)
PLEASED (4,12)
BELIEVE (2,1)
DILIGENTLY (2,4)

Hidden Title: Power of Faith

38

LABOR (14,4)
ENTER (14,13)
FALL (13,1)
SAME (8,10)
UNBELIEF (12,13)
QUICK (3,14)
SHARPER (13,7)
TWOEDGED (1,4)
PIERCING (3,7)
DIVIDING (15,9)
SOUL (9,9)
JOINTS (1,3)
DISCERNER (13,6)
INTENTS (2,12)
CREATURE (16,12)
SIGHT (4,5)
OPENED (16,14)

THEREFORE (7,9)
REST (5,13)
AFTER (7,13)
EXAMPLE (9,4)
WORD (12,12)
POWERFUL (5,1)
THAN (4,1)
SWORD (8,14)
EVEN (11,9)
ASUNDER (8,7)
SPIRIT (6,9)
MARROW (14,3)
THOUGHTS (8,2)
HEART (16,4)
MANIFEST (3,3)
THINGS (1,4)
EYES (6,6)

Hidden Title: He Sees Everything

40

GREAT (8,9)
THRONE (7,13)
EARTH (13,9)
FLED (6,12)
THERE (2,2)
PLACE (10,11)
DEAD (5,7)
STAND (2,1)
BOOKS (5,4)
OPENED (11,12)
LIFE (8,6)
THOSE (9,8)
WRITTEN (14,7)
THEIR (1,1)
GAVE (4,10)
HELL (9,5)
THEY (14,14)
CAST (1,10)
FIRE (1,11)
SECOND (1,6)

WHITE (16,9)
FACE (4,6)
HEAVEN (7,8)
AWAY (11,1)
FOUND (1,11)
THEM (11,6)
SMALL (4,2)
BEFORE (16,13)
WERE (16,4)
ANOTHER (15,1)
JUDGED (10,14)
THINGS (13,1)
ACCORDING (15,9)
WORKS (3,14)
DEATH (8,3)
DELIVERED (12,1)
EVERY (4,12)
LAKE (2,9)
THIS (2,11)
WHOSOEVER
  (15,10)

Hidden Title: Things to Come